MY DADDY DANCES TAPSTEP

Roger's Daddy's clever
Daisy's flies a plane
Michael's does computers
And has a house in Spain.
Lucy's goes to London
He stays there every week...
    But my Daddy has an earring
      and lovely dancing feet.

He hasn't got a briefcase
He hasn't got a phone
He hasn't got a mortgage
And we haven't got a home.
He hasn't got a fax machine
We haven't got a car
    But he can dance and fiddle
      And my Daddy is
        A Star.

by Peter Dixon

I LUV ME MUDDER

I luv me mudder an me mudder luvs me
We cum so far from over de sea
We heard dat de streets were paved with gold
Sometimes it's hot, sometimes it's cold,
I luv me mudder an me mudder luvs me
We try fe live in harmony
Yu might know her as Valerie
But to me she's just my mummy.

She shouts at me daddy so loud sometime
She's always been a friend of mine
She's always doing de best she can
She works so hard down ina Englan,
She's always singin sum kinda song
She has big muscles an she very, very strong,
She likes pussycats an she luv cashew nuts
An she don't bother wid no if an buts.

I luv me mudder and me mudder luvs me
We cum so far from over de sea,
We heard dat de streets were paved with gold
Sometimes it's hot, sometimes it's cold,
I luv her an whatever we do
Dis is a luv I know is true,
My people, I'm talking to yu
Me an my mudder we luv yu too.

by Benjamin Zephaniah

5

MY MUM

My mum's a chatterbox.
Her real name is Constance.
But everyone calls her Connie.
When she gets talking,
There's no stopping her.

Before she married,
Her name was Walker.
So her schoolteacher
Nicknamed her Constant Talker!

My mum's a livewire.
She's full of fun.
She's always laughing and joking.
When she gets the giggles,
There's no stopping her.

Her married name
Is Constance Wrigley.
So the neighbours have
    Nicknamed her Constant Giggly!

by John Foster

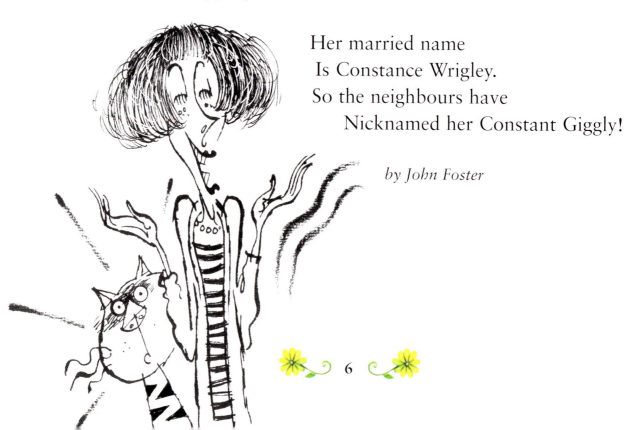

ROLLER-SKATERS

Flying by
on the winged-wheels
of their heels

Two teenage earthbirds
zig-zagging
down the street

Rising
unfeathered –
in sudden air-leap

Defying law
death and gravity
as they do a wheely

Landing back
in the smooth swoop
of youth

And faces gaping
gawking, impressed
and unimpressed

Only Mother watches – heartbeat in her mouth

by Grace Nichols

 7

THE NATIONAL UNION OF CHILDREN

NUC has just passed a weighty resolution:
'Unless all parents raise our rate of pay
This action will be taken by our members
(The resolution comes in force today):-

'Noses will not be blown (sniffs are in order),
Bedtime will get preposterously late,
Ice-cream and crisps will be consumed for breakfast,
Unwanted cabbage left upon the plate,

'Earholes and finger-nails can't be inspected,
Overtime (known as homework) won't be worked,
Reports from school will all say "Could do better",
Putting bricks back in boxes may be shirked.'

by Roy Fuller

THE NATIONAL ASSOCIATION OF PARENTS

Of course, NAP's answer quickly was forthcoming
(It was a matter of emergency),
It issued to the Press the following statement
(Its Secretary appeared upon TV):-

'True that the so-called Saturday allowance
Hasn't kept pace with prices in the shops,
But neither have, alas, parental wages:
NUC's claim would ruin kind, hard-working Pops.

'Therefore, unless the claim is now abandoned,
Strike action for us, too, is what remains;
In planning for the which we are in process
Of issuing, to all our members, canes.'

by Roy Fuller

Muuuuuuummmmmmm

Can we have a kitten
Can we have a dog
Can we call her Frisky
Can we call him Bob?
I can take him out each day
I can brush his fur
I will buy the dog meat
and milk to make her purrrr
Mum!!!

Oh...no...
Well–

Can we have a donkey
or can we have a horse
a monkey or a parrot
hamster or a snake?
Can we have a guinea pig
a peahen
or a stoat,
llama or a budgie
a rabbit or a goat?

Can we have a crocodile
gibbon or an owl,
all the zoos are closing
there's lots and lots around...
A penguin would be really good
keep it in the bath
a hyena in the garden
        to make the milkman laugh.

No, WE DON'T WANT stick insects
and goldfish aren't much fun...

Oh, can we have a puppy...
        Mum
            Mum
                Muuuuuuummmmmmmm.

by Peter Dixon

Not the dreaded photo album!

Parents! Huh!
Don't you just hate them?

You can guarantee that whenever we have visitors:
Uncle Fred, Auntie Ivy, Grandma Madge and Grandad Bill,
long lost Auntie Alice, or cousin Sidney twice removed
Mum and Dad will always, and I mean ALWAYS
get out the dreaded photo albums
and we have to sit through two and a half hours of
embarrassing snapshots of me...

stark naked in the bath with bubbles in my ears

cuddling a four foot pink fluffy teddy bear

sitting on my potty with my finger up my nose
and my nappy on my head

wearing chocolate cake like a balaclava,
cherries all over my face like extra alien eyes

the first time I tried to dress myself
with my shorts over my eyes and socks on my hands

dressed as a page boy at my Auntie's wedding
in a blue and white sailor suit and silly hat with ribbons

holding hands and kissing my posh cousin Tabatha
who has pink ribbons and flowery dresses
but never wipes her nose

blinking on every school photograph where it looks like
Mum cut my fringe with the crimping scissors

in the clothes that Mum and Dad bought me
thinking they were really trendy but were two years behind
and cheap off the market so it was okay

wearing that lovely woolly jumper that Nanna knitted
as a Christmas present using leftover wool
so that it had twenty-seven shades of green and brown
with a Thomas the Tank Engine motif
and the left arm was longer than the right.
It itched like crazy.

Everyone has a really good laugh
and I have to sit through it all tight lipped and red faced.
When I suggest that we look at last year's holiday snaps
where Mum won the knobbly knees contest
and Dad dressed up as an oven-ready turkey for the fancy dress
they tell me it's time I went to bed
and that our visitors wouldn't be interested anyway.

Parents! Huh!
Don't you just hate them?

by Paul Cookson

13

THINGS MY PARENTS SAID

Don't do as I do, do as I say.
Don't talk with your mouth full.
Children should be seen and not heard.
When you're old as I am...
Oh, how you've grown!
Eat your greens.
You want your bread buttered on both sides
And to have your cake and eat it too!
Don't forget behind the ears –
You could grow potatoes under those finger nails!
Wash your mouth out with soap and water.
It's always her and never you.
Don't throw the baby out with the bathwater.
Oh, it all goes in one ear and out the other.

by Wendy Cooling

SEEING ALL MY FAMILY

Seeing all my family
together
at special occasions
is a brilliant firework show
going off.

Grandma is a sparkler,
Grandad is a golden rain
making us brighter.
My cousins
are Catherine Wheels.
My dad is a banger
because he always talks too loud.
The best one of all
that lights up the sky
so everyone stares
is my mum
the incredible blast of sparkle
the rocket.

Every time we meet,
It always has the same effect
our family firework show.

by Claire Salama (Aged 10)

I SHARE MY BEDROOM WITH MY BROTHER

I share my bedroom with my brother
and I don't like it.
His bed's by the window
under my map of England's railways
that has a hole in just above Leicester
where Tony Sanders, he says,
killed a Roman centurion
with the Radio Times.

My bed's in the corner
and the paint on the skirting board
wrinkles when I push it with my thumb
which I do sometimes when I go to bed
sometimes when I wake up
but mostly on Sundays
when we stay in bed all morning.

That's when he makes pillow dens
under the blankets
so that only his left eye shows
and when I go deep-bed mining
for elastoplast spools
that I scatter with my feet
the night before,
and I jump on to his bed
shouting: eeyoueeyoueeyouee
heaping pillows on his head:

'Now breathe, now breathe'
and then there's quiet and silence
so I pull it away quick
and he's there laughing all over
sucking fresh air along his breathing-tube fingers.

Actually, sharing's all right.

by Michael Rosen

MEMORIES

"When I was a lad,"
Said Grandad,
"We used to play in the street.
No playing with daft computers,
But kicking a ball with bare feet."

"Aye! When I was a lass,"
Said Grandma,
"My Father worked down the pit.
And all my Mother could do for fun
Was sit and knit and knit."

by John Kitching

Now I'm just a lad
And I hold my tongue
As they talk
Of olden days.

Their memories
Of being young
Are hung in a golden
Or a dusty haze.

I don't want to argue.
I don't want to row.
I just know that I'm glad
To be living right now!

MY SISTER

My sister's just like a cat,
That's my name for her, a cat.
She's always waiting quietly,
Ready to pounce.
As soon as I do anything wrong,
She's there.
She always comes unexpectedly,
Just when I'm ready to go out –
Borrowing her dress of course.

She's always teasing,
Just like a cat teases a mouse.
A cat will chase a mouse,
Then when the mouse thinks he is getting away,
The cat will pounce.

It's not much of a life,
Having a cat following you around,
But that's what she is.
She always gets the best,
Like a cat will get the best,
The warmest place in the house.

I envy her –
I wish I was a cat.

by Susan Gowers (Aged 14)

19

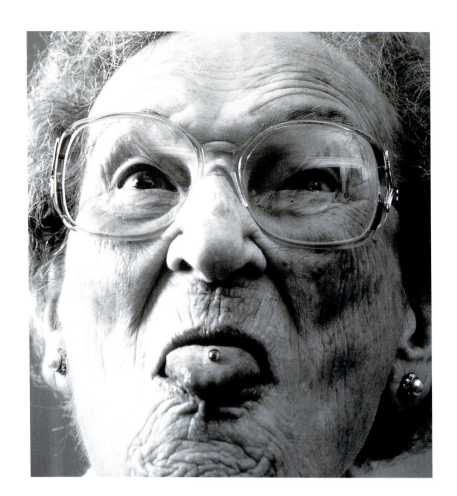

MY GRANNY IS A SUMO WRESTLER

My granny is six foot three
My granny is built like a tree
My granny says – **Nothing**
I mean nothing
Frightens me.

When Granny walks down the streets
She scares every man she meets
Nobody gonna mess with her
My granny is a Sumo Wrestler.

My granny is six foot three
My granny she's built like a tree
My granny says – **Nothing**
I mean nothing
Frightens me.

My granny does what she likes
My granny rides two motor bikes (at the same time)
My granny she breaks down doors
My granny bends bars with her jaws.

My granny she's six foot three (that's sitting down)
My granny she's built like a tree
My granny says – **Nothing**
Absolutely nothing
Frightens me.

My granny is a railway ganger
My granny is a wild head banger
My granny eats uncooked bison
My granny beat up Mike Tyson (in the first round).

My granny she's six foot three
My granny she's built like a tree (oak tree)
My granny says – **Nothing**
And I mean nothing
Ever
      Ever
            EVER
                Frightens me.

by Gareth Owen

BEST FRIENDS

It's Susan I talk to not Tracey,
  Before that I sat next to Jane;
   I used to be best friends with Lynda
    But these days I think she's a pain.

  Natasha's all right in small doses,
   I meet Mandy sometimes in town;
   I'm jealous of Annabel's pony
    And I don't like Nicola's frown.

  I used to go skating with Catherine,
   Before that I went there with Ruth;
   And Kate's so much better at trampoline:
    She's a showoff, to tell you the truth.

I think that I'm going off Susan,
She borrowed my comb yesterday;
I *think* I might sit next to Tracey,
She's my nearly best friend: she's OK.

by Adrian Henri

THE CLASSROOM CIRCLE OF FRIENDS

and I like Anne
Van likes me   → I like Anne
Dee likes Van   Anne likes Wayne
Titch likes Dee   Wayne likes Raj
Del likes Titch   Raj likes Shane
Mitch likes Del   Shane likes Paul
Ray likes Mitch   Paul likes Pam
Lai likes Ray   Pam likes Shaz
George likes Lai   Shaz likes Sam
Thai likes George   Sam likes Parv
Faye likes Thai   Parv likes Jo
Seth likes Faye   Jo likes Mick
Chris likes Seth   Mick likes Mo
Beth likes Chris   Mo likes Val
Ken likes Beth   Val likes Jill
Phil likes Ken   Jill likes Trish
Trish likes Phil

by Wes Magee

(——→ start here)

23

TRUTH

Sticks and stones may break my bones,
but words can also hurt me.
Stones and sticks break only skin,
while words are ghosts that haunt me.

Slant and curved the word-swords fall
to pierce and stick inside me.
Bats and bricks may ache through bones,
but words can mortify me.

Pain from words has left its scar
on mind and heart that's tender.
Cuts and bruises now have healed;
it's words that I remember.

by Barrie Wade

AND HOW WAS SCHOOL, TODAY?

Each day they ask: And how was school today?
Behind my mask, I shrug and say OK.

Upstairs, alone, I blink away the tears
Hearing again their scornful jeers and sneers.

Hearing again them call me by those names
As they refused to let me join their games.

Feeling again them mock me with their glares
As they pushed past me rushing down the stairs.

What have I done? Why won't they let me in?
Why do they snigger? What's behind that grin?

Each day they ask: And how was school today?
Behind my mask, I shrug and say OK.

by John Foster

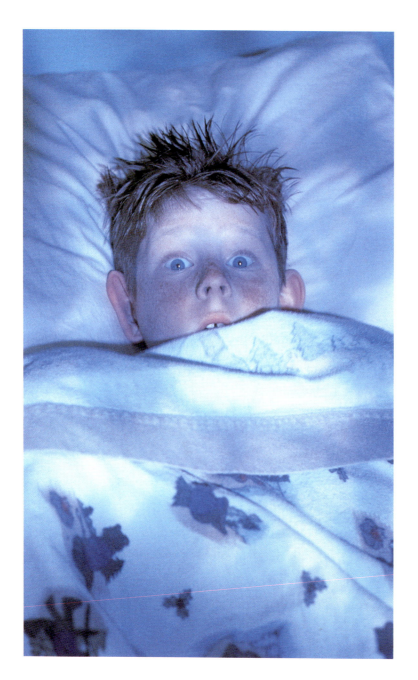

FEAR

Curling fingers
crawling up
the back
of your
brain,
taking your mind
by
surprise,
then gripping
your heart and
squeezing it
of its
life source.
A plunger
pushing
the contents
of your
stomach
down and
out.

by Deepak Kalha

Nag Nag Nag

Music – turn down
Socks – pick up
Room – tidy
Sister – play with
Answer back – don't even think about it
Consideration – have some
Know better – you should
Speak – when you're spoken to
Mouth full – don't talk with
Chores – first, play later
Piano – who wanted those lessons?
Muddy boots – not in here you don't
Feet – wipe
Friends – no homes to go to?
Computer games – you'll ruin your eyes
Biscuits – none left
Hotel – you treat this house like a
Hamster – feed
Homework – now
Nose – wipe
Bath – please take one
Ears – wash behind
Teeth – clean
Lights – out
Sleep – tight.

Mum? Yes?
Rest – give it a.

by Jane Wright

WINTER BREAK

Katie's lucky,
She's been told
to stay inside at break.
I wish I had a cold!

Ahmed's lucky.
He got only two
on Monday's spelling test.
I wish I had to stay inside
to learn the rest!

Our teacher's lucky.
Each break-time Mr. Mould
drinks coffee in the staffroom.
I wish I was old!

Each day's the same.
The sky is grey,
the wind is cold
but *still* they say,
"Off you go now,
out to play!"

It's never *me* who's told
to stay inside.
I hate it,
yes, I *hate* it,
stuck out here in the cold!

by Judith Nicholls

PARTNERS

Find a partner,
says sir, and sit
with him or her.
A whisper here,
a shuffle there,
a rush of feet.
One pair,
another pair,
till twenty-four
sit safely on the floor
and all are gone
but one
who stands,
like stone,
and waits;
tall,
still,

alone.

by Judith Nicholls

CLEAN NEW DIRTY OLD JEANS

I like jeans
blue jeans
new jeans
old jeans
gold jeans
jeans with purple polka dots

Jeans with giraffes on 'em
Jeans with lions
Jeans with elephants even
Jeans that have flies

Jeans with pockets
Jeans with rockets
Jeans with snotty comebacks on 'em

Clean jeans
painty jeans
perfectly good jeans
raggedy jeans
baggy jeans

Like I said:
new blue jeans
But best of all: old jeans
– grubby raggedy old jeans
that Mama and Papa and Grandma and Grandpa
and our school principal Harold Nyquist
just can't stand.

by Siv Widerberg

DREAM VARIATION

To fling my arms wide
In some place of the sun,
To whirl and to dance
Till the white day is done.
Then rest at cool evening
Beneath a tall tree
While night comes on gently,
    Dark like me –
That is my dream!

To fling my arms wide
In some place of the sun,
Dance! Whirl! Whirl!
Till the quick day is done.
Rest at pale evening...
A tall, slim tree...
Night coming tenderly
    Black like me.

by Langston Hughes

INDEX OF FIRST LINES

Picture credits

Cover image and title page:
Robert Harding (Michael Ventura)

Inside images:
John Birdsall pp. 5, 9, 28
Image Bank pp. 7 (A. T. Willett),
17 (Nicolas Russell), 20 (Erik Simmons)
Images Colour Library p.11
Telegraphy Colour Library p.8
(Sarah Hutchings)
Tony Stone p.14 (Eric Larrayadieu),
22 (Bill Aron), 25 (Bruno De Hogues),
26 (Donna Day)
Topham Picturepoint p.18

POEMS ABOUT RELATIONSHIPS

NEARLY BEST FRIENDS

CHOSEN BY WENDY COOLING

Illustrated by Rowan Barnes-Murphy

This edition 2003

First published in 2000 by Franklin Watts
96, Leonard Street, London EC2A 4XD

Franklin Watts Australia
45–51 Huntley Street, Alexandria NSW 2015

© Franklin Watts 2000

Editor: Sarah Snashall
Designer: Louise Thomas
Border artwork: Diana Mayo

A CIP catalogue record for this book
is available from the British Library.

ISBN 0 7496 5005 2

Dewey classification 821.008

Printed in Hong Kong/China

Acknowledgments

The editor and publishers gratefully acknowledge
permission to reproduce the following copyright material.

My Daddy Dances Tapstep, by Peter Dixon from *Peter
Dixon's Grand Prix of Poetry* (Macmillan). Reprinted by
permission of Macmillan Books. *I Luv Me Mudder*, by
Benjamin Zephaniah. Permission granted by the author. *My
Mum*, by John Foster. © 1997 John Foster (first published
in *Making Waves*, Oxford University Press). Included by
permission of John Foster. *Roller-Skaters*, by Grace Nichols.
Reproduced with permission of Curtis Brown Ltd, London
on behalf of Grace Nichols. © Grace Nichols 1994. *The
National Union of Children*, and *The National Association
of Parents*, by Roy Fuller both from *Seen Grandpa Lately?*
Andre Deutsch 1972. Permission granted by John Fuller.
Muuuuuuummmmmmm, by Peter Dixon from *Peter
Dixon's Grand Prix of Poetry* (Macmillan). Reprinted by
permission of Macmillan Books. *Not the Dreaded Photo
Album!*, by Paul Cookson. © Paul Cookson. First published
in *Parent-Free Zone*, Macmillan Books. *Seeing All My
Family*, by Claire Salama, from Wondercrup 3, edited by
Jennifer Curry (Red Fox). Reprinted by permission of
Random House. *I Share My Bedroom with My Brother*, by
Michael Rosen from *Mind Your Own Business* (Andre
Deutsch Ltd). Reprinted by permission of Scholastic Ltd.
Memories, by John Kitching. Permission granted by the
author. *My Sister*, by Susan Gowers from *Themes
Generations* (Heinemann). Permission granted by Reed
Educational and Professional Publishing. *My Granny is a
Sumo Wrestler*, by Gareth Owen. © Gareth Owen 1994.
Reproduced by permission of the author, c/o Rogers,
Coleridge & White Ltd, 20 Powis Mews, London W11
1JN. *Best Friends*, by Adrian Henri. Permission granted by
the author. *The Classroom Circle of Friends*, by Wes
Magee. Permission granted by the author. *Truth*, by Barrie
Wade. © 1987. Reprinted by permission of the author. *And
How Was School, Today?* © 1995 John Foster (first
published in *Standing on the Sidelines*, Oxford University
Press). Included by permission of John Foster. *Nag Nag
Nag*, by Jane Wright. Permission granted by the author.
Winter Break, by Judith Nicholls. © Judith Nicholls 1999.
Reprinted by permission of the author. *Partners*, by Judith
Nicholls. © Judith Nicholls 1987. From *Midnight Forest* by
Judith Nicholls, published by Faber and Faber. Reprinted by
permission of the author. *Clean New Dirty Old Jeans*, by
Siv Widerberg. Reprinted by permission of The Feminist
Press at The City University of New York, from *I'm Like
Me* by Siv Widerberg. Translated from the Swedish by
Verne Moberg. © 1968, 1969, 1970, 1971 by Siv
Widerberg. Translation © 1973 by Verne Moberg. *Dream
Variation*, by Langston Hughes. Reprinted by permission of
the author, c/o David Higham Associates, 5-8 Lower John
Street, Golden Square, London W1R 4HA.

Every effort has been made to trace copyright, but if any
omissions have been made please let us know in order that
we may put it right in the next edition.

CONTENTS